Sunrise
Sunset
52 Weeks of Awe & Gratitude

Inspirations by
Jack Canfield
Marci Shimoff
Arielle Ford
don Miguel Ruiz, Jr.
Richard Bandler
Candace Bushnell
Gloria Loring
John Bradshaw
M.J. Rose . . .

Photography by Kim Weiss

Health Communications, Inc.
Deerfield Beach, Florida

www.hcibooks.com

"Solstice Sunrise," reprinted with permission of Jeffery Armstrong. © 2014 Jeffrey Armstrong. All Rights Reserved.

Barbara Schmidt's entry excerpted from "Letting Go" section of *The Practice,* © 2014 Barb Schmidt.

Roshi Joan Halifax's entry from *www.upaya.org/dox/Boundlessly.pdf*

Rodger Kamenetz's entry excerpted from "Proverbs," from *The Lowercase Jew* (Northwestern, 2003), p.43.

Jack Canfield's entry excerpted from *Gratitude: A Daily Journal.*

Judith Orloff's entry excerpted from *The Ecstasy of Surrender.*

Dwina Gibb's entry excerpted from the poem, "My Songbird Has Flown."

**Library of Congress Cataloging-in-Publication Data
is available through the Library of Congress**

© 2014 Kim Weiss

ISBN-13: 978-07573-1808-5
ISBN-13: 978-07573-1809-2 (ePub)

Publisher: Health Communications, Inc.
        3201 S.W. 15th Street
        Deerfield Beach, FL 33442–8190

Cover image © Kim Weiss
Cover and interior design by Larissa Hise Henoch
Interior formatting by Lawna Patterson Oldfield

Dedicated to the ones I love

(sung in the key of glee)

"Now is as much bud as flower."

—Rodger Kamenetz

"Sunsets are love notes written directly to you and
last lines are always the same: Life is too short and too precious
to dwell on anything other than gratitude."

—*Gabe Berman*

Acknowledgements

Thank you to everyone who has helped me put this book together, too many to name (they are all in the book), to Peter Vegso, my longtime boss and publisher for believing in the project, to Christine Belleris, my editor (I'm so glad you're back!), Larissa Henoch for making the book more beautiful than I could have imagined, M.J. Rose for the vision of the book, and to my beloved John for inspiring this project with his gorgeous haikus written under my photographs when they only graced the pages of Facebook.

Introduction

I'm very fortunate. Living in coastal South Florida, I wake up most days and see the beautiful blue sea from my terrace. If I'm early enough, I get to witness the spectacle of the sunrise with its splashing colors and twinkling light. The same is true for the majestic sunsets I watch over to the west, as the sun slips slowly away, taking the day with it. Sometimes it feels like the sun is performing its magic just for me, sending me a message about life—a reminder that each day is unique and special.

This collection started simply. Gazing from my balcony upon Mother Nature's magnificence in a state of awe, I'd grab my camera to get "the shot" and then share my photos by email to a small group of family and friends. Then I graduated to a regular display on Facebook where, pretty quickly, my friends responded. One person remarked that the photos were like morning meditations for her, and several suggested that I turn them into a book. Without provocation, my boyfriend, John, began adding captions in the form of haikus. With corresponding words, the idea for something more permanent started to gel.

This little book was sewn together with a thread of awe coated in gratitude. Corny as that may sound, the emotions I felt—and feel—every day surprise even me. Add some beautiful words to the images, and *voila,* you have *Sunrise, Sunset: 52 Weeks of Awe & Gratitude.* Friends, colleagues, mentors, and people I've admired have generously contributed their literary impressions elicited from my sunrise and sunset photos. What I've collected from these talented people take the form of poems, affirmations, meditations, and thoughtful reflections.

I invite you to page through at your own pace and take in the vibrancy of both the pictures and the words, in any order that you like. Make it a weekly practice or devour them all at once. Nature gives me a gift every day and I share this with you.

Enjoy!

Kim

P.S. Since so many have given to me in the process of putting together this book, I am donating a portion of my proceeds to a wonderful organization, AVDA (Aid to Victims of Domestic Abuse), one that's dear to HCI.

When I was a little girl
my mother and I would play a game.
Watching a sunrise or sunset, we'd decide
which famous painter had painted the
sky that day. Sometimes it was Monet.
Or VanGogh. Or Fragonard. Or Magritte.
Sometimes it was Jackson Pollack. Or
Picasso. But always it was a masterpiece
that deserved attention and appreciation.
To this day, I play the game and am forever
grateful to her for finding such an inspired
way to teach a child about beauty and art.
Try it, the next time you see a glorious sky
. . . there's a painter up there who you'll
make smile when you guess right.

—M.J. Rose

One of my most cherished memories is of fishing on Needle Lake at the Bradshaw Ranch. Needle Lake was special because it faced the west and was boundaried by thick trees. You could literally watch the sun disappear on the horizon during the last thirty minutes of its cycle. Whether I caught fish or not, the highlight of my fishing experience was watching the sun slowly disappear on the horizon. It often sent chills down my spine and I'd always think of a stanza from one of Matthew Arnold's poems:

> Calm Soul of all things! make it mine
> To feel, amid the city's jar,
> That there abides a peace of thine,
> Man did not make, and can not mar.

—Dr. John Bradshaw, Sr.

If I hold my hands up like this, I can cup the sun in
   them just before it falls down behind the earth's edge.
Now I have a goblet of golden fire. What shall I do with it?
A moment.
A lifetime.
It's all the same.
The unbearable short sweetness of life
Makes me want to be a miserly, reckless spender of joy.
Like the sun does with its light.
An obsessive profligate,
Never wasting a second's chance to love and live with
   abandon.

—Jacob Nordby

In the Virgin Islands,

the sun has a grand old time pushing out of the sea. From my perch on a high ridge that overlooks a dozen islands, I first see the clouds on the horizon turn into golden fluff and then the sun arrives, a huge molten ball with vast pink and scarlet streamers. "Well done, old boy!" I applaud while the great dazzling orb gathers strength, parting the clouds as Moses once parted the sea. The warmth that sustains every living thing on our planet soaks beneath my skin and into my mind. Eagerly, I go forward, the new day heralded by our benevolent and blessed star.

—Homer Hickam

Every new day is another great opportunity to express my passion in life. Yesterday left, like every day before it, taking all the experiences I had on that day with it. By the grace of life, I kept the essence that allowed me to have a lifetime of experiences, my love expressed through passion. So as the sun comes up, warming my body and illuminating my path through another day of endless possibility, I take in a breath and jump into another beautiful opportunity of life.

—don Miguel Ruiz, Jr.

When I see the sun rise,
no matter what is going on in my life,
I know that life continues. Maybe
I'm grieving the loss of a close family
member or pet, or I'm anxious or
fearful of something coming up in
my day; the sunrise reminds me there
is always a new beginning. Now.
And Now. And Now.

—Joanne McCall

The night came stealing
my heart away, a billion sparkling
diamonds and the call of the coyote.
Lost in an endless eternity of questions,
only darkened clouds for paths.
The edge breaks, a golden seal, a
blazing sun announcing a new
day's miracle.

—Ann DeMarle

Even though I'm more spiritual than religious, every morning for the past thirty years I have greeted the sun with an ancient Hebrew prayer that turns my eyes and heart toward wonder, awe, and gratefulness. The chanting of these words resonates deeply in the body and leaves my heart and mind open to wonder and appreciation.

- Hebrew: מוֹדָה אֲנִי לְפָנֶיךָ מֶלֶךְ חַי וְקַיָּם שֶׁהֶחֱזַרְתָּ בִּי נִשְׁמָתִי בְּחֶמְלָה רַבָּה אֱמוּנָתֶךָ

- Transliteration: *Modah (feminine) or Modeh (masculine) ani lifanekha melekh hai v'kayom shehehezarta bi nishmahti b'hemlah rabah emunatekha.*

- Translation (more like my own version): I offer thanks to the Source of Life for returning my soul to my body for another day of life. Your compassion and faithfulness are the sacred ground upon which I stand.

—Joan Borysenko

No matter how dark the night,
out of the billions and billions of stars . . .
it is always our own bright star
that pierces the darkness
and brings a new day.

—Richard Bandler

Sunrise brings a chance to begin again, to smooth ruffled feathers, quiet doubt, and once more consider the possibility of joy.

Sunset is an exhalation, a softening of the day's intent, as our plans and schemes slip into the deep dreams of the heart.

—Gloria Loring

We stand in awe at the benevolence of the universe. For a brief moment, we are pardoned from the frantic pace that exists in our world. All time seems to stand still. In the presence of this majestic, glittering, golden sunset, we are filled with gratitude, embraced in this magical moment of holy communion.

—Janet Bray Attwood

Every sunrise is an invitation to what could turn out to be the best party ever. Dress for it and pack a snack—just in case you feel peckish—and you're sure to have a least a little fun that day.

Watching a sunset makes me feel warm and surrounded by love, and a part of a fabulous adventure that's just beginning. Plus it means there's cake in the offing.

I've never met a sunset I didn't like. It means dinner's almost ready.

—Frank De Caro

For every set of eyes that see the morning sun,
There is a mind, a heart, and, for some, a soul.

The camera of the mind reflects awe and gratitude
for a willing bank of moments and memories,
of that golden, molten star that gives us light.

Then comes a feeling in the power of the heavens,
there to record how little we know

But how sure we love the star,
that drenches us in warmth and wonder.

—Bill Finley

At the start of a fresh new day, there is a feeling that yesterday is gone, and up ahead there are great opportunities. With this sense of renewal, all things are possible.

—Dawn Maslar

Imagine that the sunrise unfolding in front of you is a divine portal of wisdom. And although too intense to take it all in at once, by relaxing, the warmth of wisdom will flood over you.

—Gary Bello

May each new sunrise give you the gift of awakening into the vibrant life you are so destined to live. An amazing sunrise reminds us so clearly how nature has given so brilliantly to us while asking very little in return. In this sacred humility, the sunrise says, *"Breathe, Believe—and most importantly—BE LIFE."*

—Reverend Temple Hayes

SUNRISE: Is anyone out there? Can anyone hear me? What kind of day will I have? Will I meet someone special today? Can I really improve my health? Wouldn't it be great to travel the world? I squint my eyes into the morning sun and see all sorts of dancing images and receive all sorts of answers. Yes, the good and hopeful answers always come at sunrise.

—Dorothy Breininger

I can't think of anything except sunrise at my house—when it sets the tops of the trees on fire I know it's going to be a glorious day.

—Candace Bushnell

I once had a bedroom where I could see the sunrise through one window and the sunset through another. Mornings, I'd watch the sun spread its orange butter thicker and thicker around the oak trees, and then brilliantly dissolve in a flood of growing light. Evenings I'd sit in awe as the sky played with the sun's box of crayons. These sacred bookends of light and color always lifted my heart and filled me with gratitude for the beauty of both beginnings and endings.

—HeatherAsh Amara

The sun is setting and I feel once again transfixed by the wonder of its pinkish glow. Lost in a quiet kind of awe. I have lived and loved for one more day. What I have done is done. What I have said is said. What I have lived is lived. This day is finished, the day is done. I let go of what needs letting go of, resolve to give my best to tomorrow and tuck myself into the reassuring arms of God as I glide into an unconscious and revitalizing world of rest, knowing that tomorrow, the sun will rise again. This is my world, I belong here.

—Tian Dayton, Ph.D.

The rising sun, the morning star, a new day. In the Andes, the Q'ero people meet each morning with their prayers, light from light. There is a tradition I brought home from my times in Peru. Facing the sun we open up our bodies, outstretched arms, palms facing forward, breathing deep and slow, and exhaling all attachments. Breathing in light, bringing our right hand over our hearts, saying aloud, "With all my love," then the left hand over the area just beneath the belly button and saying aloud, "With no fear, I meet the day." May peace be with you.

—Lee McCormick

Reflect no more on the tides of yesterday
The state of independent thought
Lies only upon the width of a paper's edge
One side cannot be reborn
The other as yet unseen
Now in the tempest of this moment
Do the clouds of confusion disintegrate

—Robin Hill

Sunrises really speak to me. They say, "Hey buddy, look at this day I'm giving you. Don't screw it up. Work hard. Play nice. Trust your heart. Be brave, but don't be stupid. Share your mercy and your smile. Then rest and eat with those you love. And I'll bring you more sunshine in the morning."

—Sean Kenniff, M.D.

I brood. I contemplate. I crouch anxiously behind the thousand things I think I should do and I think I should be. It all feels So Important.

Then I accidentally witness an exquisitely resplendent sun kissing the glittering horizon. Maybe after anguished hours of insomnia, it catches me off guard through an open window. Or maybe it startles me on my way across a gravel parking lot after a disheartening afternoon meeting. A sunrise. A sunset.

And if I remember to stop, if I recognize the calling, it releases me. If only I let it, the radiant blaze sizzles away my artificial busy-ness, unfurrows my purposeful brow, and strips me down to WHO I AM.

The awareness seeps up from my bones: Drenched in mystery and excruciating promise, this impossibly perfect sky is never before and never again. Just like me.

—Lisa McCourt

Make a conscious

decision to have an attitude of gratitude. Choose to live in a state of constant joy, gratitude, and appreciation, and acknowledge how fortunate you are. Don't take even the simplest things for granted—appreciate them and give thanks. This feeling and expression of gratitude is simply good for you. It increases your sense of well-being, awareness, enthusiasm, happiness, determination, and optimism. It raises your vibrational frequency and creates an upward-spiraling process of ever increasing joy, gratitude, and abundance that just keeps getting better and better.

—Jack Canfield

The day was winding down on Waikiki Beach, families packing up, kids begging for a few more minutes in the ocean. My moments of quiet reflection were pleasantly distracted by increasing numbers of people coming off the street to gather on the sand and under the palms, softly chatting, watching as the sun dipped lower, lower. As the edge of the sun fell below the horizon, the now-large crowd erupted in cheers and applause, celebrating a magnificent performance and the next turn in a cycle that connects us all.

—Jane Bluestein, Ph.D.

Stand tall with your feet on
the ground, feel the earth under your
feet and raise your head towards the sun.
Take in its warmth and carry it with you.
When you feel cold with fear, when
you feel alone and lost, look to the sun,
close your eyes and let it warm your
heart, let it feed your soul, let it remind
you of your divinity.

—Betsy Chasse

The Christian myth of the birth of the Holy Child is an extraordinarily powerful rite of passage. Its power in part is in the death of the old sun, the old time, the old way of being, and the birth of a new sun, a new time, a new way of being. It tells of the coming of a wondrous child out of the darkness of the age and the womb and his entry into an illuminated life of Great Time. Once this occurs, the world turns a corner. Everything is changed, different, re-sourced. In participating in the myth of the new sun and the Holy Child, you may even feel born within yourself options, possibilities, opportunities, both remarkable and renewing. Thus the enormous power of this story, for what can be more powerful and more evocative than the child? Here is a potency deeper than all our fears, more basic than all our everyday conditionings. It's stronger than our ego constructs, a flowing cornucopia of that which never was but is always happening.

—Jean Houston

53

Sunrise and sunset,

the bookends of my daily life, are the moments when I am most drawn to God.

I know that sunrise is the only letter of introduction we get for life's opportunities; it reminds me to live every day as a God-given opportunity for greatness because tomorrow it may be someone else's challenge.

Sunrise impresses upon me the need to deposit a lot of happiness in the bank account of memories, as well as the courage to live up to my divine responsibility to help make this a better world in order to justify my having been created.

—Rabbi Benjamin Blech

My songbird has flown and the world sighs
The veil of night has fallen
But a dawn of the Divine will rise for a new day
My songbird has flown and the world sighs
But we know that he is never far away.

—Dwina Gibb

When I look at a sunrise, I am grateful for beginnings. Each new day is God's gift, filled with new opportunities. He fills each morning with light and a myriad of soft colors, so that we approach each challenge or decision with clarity and a palette of perspective. In the new light of day, I pray that the Almighty not only gives me clarity, but the courage to live it.

—Lori Palatnik

I like to think of the sun as my role model: sharing warmth, light, and life with all beings without discriminating as to who deserves it. I love to meditate at sunrise when the spiritual power of the sun is the strongest. I can feel the blessings of Spirit and I know that the sun awakens the seeds God has planted inside me to grow and thrive.

—Barbara Biziou

The sages asked,

"Who is rich?" and answered,
"That person who rejoices in their lot."

Gratitude.

Sometimes, it takes practice.

We can be grateful for the obvious
blessings of family, shelter, a job, a car,
food, and clothing. How about our eyes,
ears, nose, mouth, legs, fingers, etc.?

Even that cup of coffee we enjoy while checking
our emails or watching the sun rise.

More than anything, we can appreciate
the fact that we have so much to
appreciate . . . and appreciate that!

—Bob Burg

This day is now over.
I choose to live in the present moment.
I am thankful for having been given this
day and the blessing that it has held.
I take comfort in now releasing any
challenges or successes I experienced
today, and I head into a restful sleep
with the peace and knowledge that
tomorrow is a new day. I am always
working toward the person I wish to be.

—Barb Schmidt

63

As a lifelong early riser, I must admit that sunrise is my favorite time of day. It signals new beginnings, a blank slate with no mistakes—yet. And it reminds me that, as the Bible says in the Book of Lamentations, God's mercies are new every morning. Sunset is a time to reflect on what I have done with the time I've been given. Each day is a sort of mini lifetime.

Three years ago, I was diagnosed with multiple myeloma—a cancer they told me was incurable, but that could achieve remission. From that moment on, remission became my mission. I had no idea then the battle I was in for. Today, one year into that remission, every sunrise reminds me to thank God for each new day. He has renewed my contract! Life is not to be taken for granted. Hug your loved ones often and be thankful for what you have. There are no guarantees.

—Pat Williams

People have worshiped the self-luminous star at the center of our solar system from the beginning of time, rendering it divine. It's been said that the surrendering mind creates divinity and that anything you surrender to becomes a god or a place of holiness. Surrender to the beauty of nature today by standing in awe before the rising sun or paying homage to a sunset. Remember, nature's way is the way of perfection.

—Alexandra Katehakis

Just before dawn, I love to awaken to the birds' cheerful song, look out at the clouds shimmering pink and gold on the horizon, and stand mesmerized as the sun miraculously rises. Sunrise is my favorite time of day—the air is still, yet filled with potential. A fresh vibrancy wakes up my cells; a curiosity for what's ahead rouses my spirit. Every morning, we get another chance to live our best day and to witness the mystery of life unfolding.

—Marci Shimoff

Sunrises have always meant glorious hope and endless possibilities to me ever since I was a little girl. I feel immensely uplifted as if each day has an Easter message being given to us by God. We are not alone, we are protected and we are dearly, dearly loved. With so much love and strength behind us, we can do anything and those dreams we have dreamed all night for ourselves, in the day can become reality.

—Catherine Lanigan

holy morning

I am called into the quiet
by my reverence for life
and my yearning
to once again fully embrace
my life
to dwell in the sweetness
of just this moment
and be filled with the light
of a new day rising

—Minx Boren

What I love most about sunrises and sunsets, in addition to their incredible beauty, is that they touch a deeper chord in us, a primal one that reaches far into the memory banks of the DNA and viscerally reminds us of the ongoing cycle of life. Breath-giving more than breath-taking.

—Steven Farmer, Ph.D.

Thank you, sun. You give us life, warmth, so that even in the shadows of night we long for morning. In the morning we long for night. Sunrises and sunsets, then, are the heralds of our desires, calling us forward to new tomorrows, forever revolving around a super-heated ball of fire. From it, comes all the energy to fuel our planet's life. What should we fear, then, if we are all children of flame, of light. Every time you disappear, a tiny part of me fears you will never return. But you always, always do.

So imagine what it will feel like to watch the sunrise on your last day of life. Imagine that *this* is that sunrise. Now go and live your day, remembering how precious is every moment of light.

—J. Gabriel Gates

In your life, you can call on the energy of the wind to clear blocks from your system. Be aware of the soft breeze caressing your face, allowing that gentleness in. Also, go outdoors during gusty winds without resisting them. Let the surge of air rush through you and muss up your hair. Feel yourself getting lighter, more youthful, carefree. Imagine your fears and troubles being purged, no longer a burden. The wind can help you let go if you want. Consciously surrender your struggles to the wind, in gratitude.

—Judith Orloff, M.D.

As my morning coffee mists my face, the sunrise melts my heart with its violets, tangerines, pale pinks, and rich golds splashed across the mountains. One of the most amazing things, for me, is knowing that I'm connected to every other person on the Earth. My destiny is as caught up in that of a mother of six, who dwells in a slum in Nairobi and scavenges for street food in the early dawn, as it is to an eleven-year-old Honduran boy, who's up at first light to fetch heavy buckets of water miles away. Wherever we rise each day, it's comforting—and empowering—to know we're all wrapped in the sun's hopeful, shimmering light. And that, once again, that red ball is rising in the sky declaring, "Anything is possible today!"

—Susan Skog

Mind:

be a vast, clear sky—
a crystalline vessel
that reflects the great sun.
Dispel the darkness,
shine with equanimity
on each and every one
regardless of
   culture
   creed
   color
   morality
   belief
   or disbelief.
When thick thought-clouds form
and the discordant rumble of
my anger and discontent threaten
to strike and harm others,
may the indestructible sun within
burn away the fog of my ignorance
to reveal my true, original nature.

—Melissa L. Applegate

My beloved soulmate Brian declared a long time ago that we should never miss a sunset and it's rare that we do. Most of the time, we stand on our deck watching that incredible golden ball of light as it sinks into the deep blue Pacific Ocean. We stand enchanted as we pinch ourselves at the magnificence of the event and all of our blessings.

—Arielle Ford

Let's lead with love . . . follow your heart's intelligence . . . Get out there and dance—get out there and do the Leela! . . . Catch some waves—if you "wipe out" get back up and catch another one . . . PARTICIPATE in life as it unfolds in ALL its glory and joy . . . Live it and breathe it all in fully heart and soul—even when we feel the angst, the pain and despair . . . take it all in cause life is too short!

—Brian Hilliard

This is the day the Lord has made, I rejoice as I move forward to do what needs to be done by me. I know that my way is made clear, safe, happy, and successful. My heart and mind are filled with gratitude!

—Rev. Nancy Norman

What if the sun set and rose every ten years? Everyone would run out to observe and declare the beauty of the day! We would relish every minute of that day. It would be nothing but beauty all day long. Everything we gazed upon would cause our hearts to rejoice! . . . The sun rose today. Today is the one day given to you . . . relish it and sing its praises!

—Rev. Cathy Jean Norman

Solstice Sunrise

The summer light
Lasted half the night
When the Solstice had just gone by,
The electric blue
Cast an eerie hue
Like a soul that will never die.

On a golden mountain,
A silver fountain
Sends forth streams of light,
Beneath towering trees,
With jewels for leaves,
Flows the river of my delight

And that day shines yet,
Now it will not set,
In my heart, either night or day
But once in a while
On my joyful smile,
You can glimpse that eternal ray.

—Jeffrey Armstrong

The first rays of light spur me to remember the short dash between life and death and make the most of it. I've had a lifelong practice of wanting to stay on the sunshine side of the mountain as long as possible each day in both attitude and action.

Sunset reminds me of our family motto: Live for today, plan for tomorrow, no regrets. My beloved wife of thirty-five years, Teresa, and I not only don't go to bed mad, we always face each other and hold hands as we go to sleep.

—Marty Becker, D.V.M.

We see that space is boundless and without boundary; this is the wondrous freedom of openness, no hindrance, our natural freedom, the spirit and mind of inclusiveness. And our connection with all beings and things is boundless and without boundary as well; this is the wonder of our interdependence, how we live in a seamless world of connections, Indra's net: each jewel reflecting the light of all others, held together in a weave of space and connectivity.

— Roshi Joan Halifax

I realize I've seen many more sunsets in my life than sunrises. As I get older, I propose to myself a new delicacy: waking up earlier, facing the birth of fire in the east to balance the dazzling light shows of the west.

The earth, the seasons, and the changing of the light are my oldest companions. The sky outside of me is also inside of me. I am learning to listen to its whisper. It says to me: "Life is huge. Paint with every color in your wild palette of aliveness."

—Luisa Kolker

The beach has always been my respite from the activity of daily life. I recall when I was younger that we sometimes went before the sunrise. Sitting quietly on the sand we waited patiently until it seemed that even on a somber day, somehow we urged the sun above the waves. It never lasted long enough, the sunrise itself, but as the sun rose and filled the sky it seemed to lift our cares away as well. Returning home refreshed and glowing from the warmth, we realized that once again our lives were full and bright.

—Jennifer Arnold Klein, M.D.

When I look at the brilliant colors of the sunset it's as if the universe is rewarding me for a day of serving, saying, "Job well done."

The color red honors and acknowledges the fire in my belly, my strength and power.

Orange celebrates my bright light and acknowledges my community; I realize I am but a piece of a much larger plan.

Yellow-gold is the healing color that warms and restores my soul so I may lay down and relax from trying to do it all.

Sunset is a hug.
Sunset is a kiss.
It holds me in its arms and I am in awe.

—Lisa Nichols

As I open my eyes, I slowly sit up and contemplate my day. I see the light creeping in through the window, the particles dancing around the room.

I follow their patterns.

I stretch my arms, feeling the reluctance of my bones to leave this comfy bed.

My mind begins to twirl and I feel the anxiety in my chest as I remember the undone tasks, the obligations and appointments that I need to fulfill.

Is this the way I want to begin this day?

I exhale deeply and relax. I am the co-creator of my life.

This subtle energy manifests throughout my body. It holds the infinite possibility that these next few hours hold for me. How do I want to use them? What will I make of this day before me? I deliberately and mindfully choose to experience fun, joy, and delight this day. I will carve out time to work and treat myself with something splendid before the day is over. Like a child eager to go play, I direct my energy and enthusiasm in ways that celebrate life!

—Rokelle Lerner

Sunrise

"Today" is a new day, a new beginning, a new chapter. I connect with the Divine as a child connecting with the parent in love. I am protected, and filled with fresh hope and enthusiasm. Looking at the ocean, I remember I am a lighthouse sharing the light of Love and the light of Truth with all. Keeping this in my awareness, I will use my thoughts, words, and actions to share this light with each one I connect with today.

Sunset

At the end of the day, check: Am I at peace with myself, with others and the world?

I remind myself that whatever has happened has been part of the eternal world drama. Everything was filled with deep significance and was accurate. I am content and peaceful.

I ask myself: What would I have done differently today? As the whole film flashes in front of me, I see the good, and I surrender it to the Divine to keep myself free from ego.

I see the things that were not so good, learn the lessons from them and move on . . .

—Sister Jayanti, Brahma Kumaris

Contributor Bios

Amara, HeatherAsh
Author of *The Toltec Path of Transformation* and *Warrior Goddess Training* and founder of Toci-The Toltec Center of Creative Intent. *www.heatherashamara.com*

Applegate, Melissa
Author, *The Egyptian Book of Life: Symbolism of Ancient Egyptian Temple and Tomb Art,* intuitive counselor, meditation instructor and Feng Shui consultant based in Palm Springs, Florida.

Armstrong, Jeffrey
Award-winning author of, *God the Astrologer,* visionary, spiritual teacher, founder of the Vedic Academy of Sciences and Arts, English literature, history, and comparative religions. He studied Sanskrit and has a vast knowledge of Ayurveda, Jyotisha, and many of the related historical Vedic texts. *www.jeffreyarmstrong.com*

Atwood, Janet Bray
New York Times bestselling author of *The Passion Test: The Effortless Path to Discovering Your Life Purpose. www.thepassiontest.com*

Bandler, Richard
Author of *Get the Life You Want, Richard Bandler's Guide to Trance-formation,* and co-developer of Neuro-Linguistic-Programming (NLP). *www.richardbandler.com*

Borysenko Ph.D., Joan
Cell biologist, psychologist, spiritual educator and *New York Times* bestselling author of *Minding the Body Mending the Mind* and 15 other books. *www.joanborysenko.com*

Becker D.V.M., Marty
"America's Veterinarian," contributor to ABC-TV's *Good Morning America,* resident veterinarian on *The Dr. Oz Show* and pet expert for AARP. He is co-author of *Chicken Soup for the Pet Lover's Soul* and practices veterinary medicine at the North Idaho Animal Hospital. *www. drmartybecker.com*

Bello, Gary
Author of *Enlightening Moments,* public speaker, interfaith minister, therapist, and coach, with a full-time practice of yoga and meditation since 1971. Developer of a system that integrates the ancient wisdom of India with modern body mind psychology and holistic therapies. *www. garyandradhabello.com*

Berman, Gabe
Author, *Live Like a Fruit Fly. www.omgabe.wordpress.com*

Blech, Rabbi Benjamin
Professor of Talmud, Yeshiva University, author of 15 bestselling books including *Why Is God Good but the World So Bad,* and frequent contributor to major publications. *www. benjaminblech.com*

Biziou, Barbara
Author of *The Joy of Ritual* and *The Joys of Family Rituals,* integrates her extensive knowledge of global spiritual practices, rituals, psychology, and business into her coaching and consulting practice. She is the renowned go-to expert for high-end, custom ceremonies, global rituals, weddings, and the celebration of all life's passages. *www.joyofritual.com*

Bluestein, Ph.D., Jane
Jane is an award-winning author whose books include *Creating Emotionally Safe Schools; High School's Not Forever; Parents, Teens and Boundaries; The Parent's Little Book of Lists; Mentors, Masters, and Mrs. McGregor: Stories of Teachers Making a Difference;* and *Magic, Miracles and Synchronicity: A Journal of Gratitude and Awareness. www.janebluestein.com*

Boren, Minx
Author of *Healing Is a Journey* and four books of poetry, Master Certified Coach and facilitator of innovative programs that support health and balance, reflection, and achievement. *www.coachminx.com*

Breininger, Dorothy
Author of *Stuff Your Face or Face Your Stuff* and expert organizer on the Emmy-nominated series, *Hoarders.* She created the "Curb the Chaos" System, which helps individuals conquer their clutter in a pleasing and fun way. *www.dorothytheorganizer.com*

Bradshaw, Sr., Dr. John
Called "America's leading personal growth expert," he is the author of five *New York Times* bestsellers, *Bradshaw On: The Family, Healing the Shame That Binds You, Homecoming, Creating Love,* and *Family Secrets.* John's books have sold over 4 million copies in North America and he has hosted several programs for PBS. *www.johnbradshaw.com*

Burg, Bob
Professional speaker and author of the international bestsellers, *Endless Referrals* and *The Go-Giver.* His newest book is *Adversaries into Allies. www.burg.com*

Bushnell, Candace
American novelist and television producer based in New York City. Raised in Connecticut, she wrote a column for the *New York Observer* from 1994 to 1996, which was adapted into the best-selling *Sex and the City* anthology. *www.candacebushnell.com*

Canfield, Jack
Author, speaker, trainer, and originator of the *Chicken Soup for the Soul™* series, the *Success Principles* series, and America's leading authority on creating success and personal fulfillment. *www.jackcanfield.com*

Chasse, Betsy
Author, filmmaker, and co-creator of the film *What The Bleep Do We Know?!* Books include including *Tipping Sacred Cows, Metanoia: A Transformative Change of Heart* and the companion book to *BLEEP. Zentropy* is her recent documentary film. *www.betsychasse.net*

Dayton, Ph.D., Tian
Clinical psychologist, prolific author, and nationally recognized expert in the fields of psychodrama and addictions. Recent books include *One Foot in Front of the Other* and *Emotional Sobriety: From Relationship Trauma to Resilience and Balance. www.tiandayton.com*

De Caro, Frank
Host of his own live national talk show, *The Frank De Caro Show,* daily on Sirius XM Satellite Radio. He is the author of four books including *The Dead Celebrity Cookbook. www.frankdecaro.com*

De Marle, Ann
Associate Dean at Champlain College, directing its Emergent Media Center, Masters of Fine Arts in Emergent Media, and Master of Science in Emergent Media in Shanghai, China. Founder of the Game Development and the Multimedia undergraduate degrees, recipient of the Roger H. Perry Endowed Chair. *demarle.blogspot.com/*

Farmer, Steven
Licensed psychotherapist, shamanic practitioner, ordained minister and author of *Animal Spirit Guides, Earth Magic®, Earth Magic® Oracle Cards,* and the *Children's Spirit Animal Cards.* He offers a certification program, the Earth Magic® Practitioner training. *www.earthmagic.com*

Finley, Bill
Author, *Curing Urbanitis, Air Force Cowboy,* and *Shaking Up Boca*. Retired planning and development professional and World War II bomber pilot.

Ford, Arielle
Bestselling author of eight books, including: *Wabi Sabi Love* and *The Soulmate Secret*. Ford is a leading personality in the personal growth and contemporary spirituality movement. She is a radio host, relationship expert, speaker, columnist and blogger for the *Huffington Post*. *www.arielleford.com*

Gates, J. Gabriel
Author of the horror novel *The Sleepwalkers,* YA fantasy novels *Dark Territory, Ghost Crown,* and *Shadow Train,* and the sci-fi thriller *Blood Zero Sky. www.jgabrielgates.com*

Gibb, Dwina
Irish playwright, poet, artist and author of a trilogy about Cormac mac Airt, a second century High King in Ireland; two Regency Mystery novels: *Pandora's Dilemma* and *The Lady's Dilemma.* Poetry: "Ergot on the Rye"; "Love Unbound." Comedic Plays: "Last Confessions of a Scallywag"; "The Divil at the Fingerpost"; "The Gabby Aggies." *www.dwinagibb.co.uk*

Halifax, Roshi Joan
American Zen Buddhist roshi, anthropologist, ecologist, civil rights activist, hospice caregiver, and the author of several books on Buddhism and spirituality. She currently serves as abbot and guiding teacher of Upaya Zen Center in Santa Fe, New Mexico. *www.upaya.org*

Hayes, Temple
Spiritual leader, author, radio host, motivational speaker, ordained Unity Minister and CEO of First Unity campus (St. Petersburg, Florida). Books include: *When Did You Die, The Right to Be You* and *How to Speak Unity. www.templehayes.com*

Hickam, Homer
American author, Vietnam veteran, and a former NASA engineer. His autobiographical novel *Rocket Boys: A Memoir,* was a number one *New York Times* bestseller and the basis for the 1999 film *October Sky.* Hickam has also written a number of bestselling memoirs and novels including the "Josh Thurlow" historical fiction novels. *www.homerhickam.com*

Hill, Robin
Professional photographer specializing in architecture, and owner and photographer of Robin Hill Photography. *www.robinhill.net*

Hilliard, Brian
Has spent the last 25 years developing, managing, and investing in commercial real estate, telecommunications, publishing, film, and music entertainment properties. His primary focus is on humanitarian projects and assisting nonprofit organizations in fundraising, business consulting, and hands-on participation. *www.facebook.com/brian.hilliard.9?fref=ts*

Houston, Jean
Scholar, philosopher, and researcher in Human Capacities and one of the principal founders of the Human Potential Movement. A prolific writer, Dr. Houston is the author of 26 books including *Jump Time, A Passion for the Possible, Search for the Beloved, Life Force, The Possible Human, Public Like a Frog, A Mythic Life: Learning to Live Our Greater Story,* and *Manual of the Peacemaker. www.jeanhouston.org*

Jayanti, Sister
Director of the Brahma Kumaris World Spiritual Organization, London, and based at their Global Cooperation House in London, United Kingdom. She is the European director of the Brahma Kumaris World Spiritual University, assists in coordinating the university's activities in over 80 countries, and is the BKWSU's representative to the United Nations, Geneva. *brahmakumaris.info/w/index.php?title=Sister_Jayanti*

Katahakis, Alexandra
Founder of the Center for Healthy Sex in Los Angeles, California, and author of *Erotic Intelligence: Igniting Hot Healthy Sex After Recovery from Sex Addiction. www.centerforhealthysex.com*

Kamenetz, Rodger
Award-winning poet, author, and teacher. Of his ten books, his best known is *The Jew in the Lotus.* Other Kamenetz titles include: *This History of Last Night's Dream, Burnt Books* and *Stalking Elijah. www.rodgerkamenetz.com*

Kenniff, M.D., Sean
Neurologist and author of the book, *Etre the Cow* and *Stop Effing Yourself,* and one of the original contestants on *Survivor,* the prime-time series. *www.etrethecow.com*

Klein, M.D., Jennifer Arnold
Neonatologist for Texas Children's Hospital and assistant professor of pediatrics-neonatology at Baylor College of Medicine in Houston, she co-stars with her husband Bill in the TLC series *The Little Couple. www.jenniferarnoldmd.com*

Kolker, Luisa, M.A.. L.P.C.C.
Licensed psychotherapist and shamanic healer. Luisa facilitates seasonal earth-based ceremonies and private sessions. She has developed and teaches two dynamic somatic-shamanic healing models, *The Transformation Process* and *The 3 Energy Body Model. www.luisakolker.com*

Catherine Lanigan
Author of over 30 books including: *The Evolving Woman: True Confessions of Surviving Mr. Wrong; Angel Watch, Divine Nudges* and *Wings of Destiny.* Her newest series of romances is *Shores of Indian Lake; Love Shadows* and *Heart's Desire. A Fine Year for Love, Lost Love* and *Unbridled Love* is next. *www.catherinelanigan.com*

Lerner, Rokelle
Psychotherapist, international consultant and lecturer. Books include *The Object of My Affection Is in My Reflection, Daily Affirmations for Adult Children of Alcoholics, Affirmation for the Child Within* and more. Co-creator and facilitator of the InnerPath Programs for Cottonwood Tucson. *www.rokellelerner.com*

Loring, Gloria
Author of *Coincidence Is God's Way of Remaining Anonymous,* actress, recording artist of the number one hit song "Friends and Lovers;" co-composer of TV theme songs, and beloved as "Liz Chandler" on *Days of Our Lives.* Spokesperson for the Juvenile Diabetes Research Foundation. *www.glorialoring.com*

Maslar, Dawn
Author of *Your Hearts Desire,* biologist, professor, and "science of love" expert. Maslar resides in South Florida. *www.dawnmaslar.com*

McCall, Joanne
The Media Polisher and founder of Media Boot Camp.*www.themediapolisher.com*

McCormick, Lee
Author of *Spirit Recovery Medicine Bag, Spirit Recovery Journal,* and founder and co-owner of the Ranch Recovery Center in Tennessee. He founded Spirit Recovery, Inc., which produces recovery conferences, sacred journeys, workshops, and other recovery and personal growth experiences. *www.spiritrecovery.com*

McCourt, Lisa
An award-winning editorial director, publishing executive, and author with over 6 million books sold, including *I Love You Stinky Face,* the *Chicken Soup for the Little Soul* series and her book for adults, *Juicy Joy: Seven Simple Steps to Your Glorious, Gutsy Self. www.lisamccourt.com*

Miguel Ruiz, Jr., don
Author of *The Five Levels of Attachment,* Ruiz Jr. apprenticed with his renowned father, don Miguel Ruiz in the Toltec tradition and now helps others discover optimal physical and spiritual health. *www.miguelruizjr.com*

Nichols, Lisa
CEO of Motivating the Masses, one of the top training and development companies in the world, one of the most sought-after transformational speakers with a global platform, and a bestselling author of six books, including co-authoring *Chicken Soup for the African-American Soul. www.motivatingthemasses.com*

Nordby, Jacob
Author, speaker, and creativity coach who accidentally sparked a worldwide phenomenon when he wrote and shared: "Blessed are the weird people: poets, misfits, writers, mystics, heretics, painters and troubadours—for they teach us to see the world through different eyes." He is author of *The Divine Arsonist: A Tale of Awakening. www.jacobnordby.com*

Norman, Revs. Cathy and Nancy
Nancy Norman is the minister of Unity of Delray Beach (Florida) and her daughter, Cathy Jean Norman, is the minister of Unity Church of Ventura (California). Both have been with Unity Church for many years and Cathy holds the distinction of having been the youngest minister ordained by the organization.*www.unityofdelraybeach.org* and *www.unityofventura.org*

Orloff, Judith
Psychiatrist, intuitive healer, and *New York Times* bestselling author. Her latest book is *The Ecstasy of Surrender: 12 Surprising Ways Letting Go Can Empower Your Life.* Dr. Orloff's other bestsellers are *Emotional Freedom, Second Sight, Positive Energy,* and *Intuitive Healing. www.drjudithorloff.com*

Palatnik, Lori
Author, speaker, and media personality, is the founding director of the Jewish Women's Renaissance Project *(jwrp.org),* which created a "Birthright" for Jewish women, bringing thousands of mothers to Israel each year, from 18 different countries, for an eight-day transformational experience. *www.aish.com/sp/lal/*

Rose, M.J.
M.J. Rose believes books that exaggerate mystery and magic draw attention to it and remind us to look for it and revel in it. Her latest is *The Collector of Dying Breaths* in her *Reincarnationist* series. Rose is also founder of the first marketing company for authors: *AuthorBuzz.* And she is the inspiration for the structure and words that fill this book. *www.mjrose.com*

Schmidt, Barb
Author, *The Practice* and founder of Peaceful Mind Peaceful Life, a nonprofit organization that works with the Peace Studies Department at Florida Atlantic University (FAU) in Boca Raton, Florida. With FAU, Schmidt has hosted presentations by HH Dali Lama, Doris Kearns Goodwin, Gabrielle Bernstein, and more, to further her mission for world peace. *www.barbschmidt. com*

Skog, Susan
Journalist, activist, humanitarian and author of, *The Give-Back Solution: Create a Better World with Your Time, Talents, and Travel, Peace in our Lifetime,* and *Embracing Our Essence: Spiritual Conversations with Prominent Women.* In her work, Skog has supported the efforts of more than 30 organizations easing extreme poverty in the developing world. *www.susanskog.com*

Williams, Pat
Prolific author, motivational speaker, and sports executive, currently serving as a senior vice president of the NBA's Orlando Magic. *www.patwilliams.com*